RUBÁIYÁT · OF OMAR · KHAYYÁM

RUBÁIYÁT · OF · OMAR · KHAYYÁM

RENDERED INTO ENGLISH VERSE
BY EDWARD FITZGERALD
WITH ILLUSTRATIONS BY
· EDMUND DULAC ·

INTRODUCTION BY
A. S. BYATT

QUALITY PAPERBACK BOOK CLUB
NEW YORK

INTRODUCTION

✦

I grew up with my head full of Victorian poetry. I had illustrated editions of Tennyson's *Lady of Shalott* and *Morte d'Arthur* as painting books, and can still recite most of both of them. Not only that, they haunt my writing—at moments of passion or despair in my early novels, I would recognize a ghost of a rhythm—"Out flew the web, and floated wide/The mirror cracked from side to side"—or Sir Bedivere's armed footsteps "clanging" on the side of the mere—in the sentence I was about to write. Understanding of life came through poems—*In Memoriam* gave thrilling form to fears and doubts:

> So runs my dream: but what am I?
> An infant crying in the night:
> An infant crying for the light:
> And with no language but a cry.

I came to FitzGerald's *Rubáiyát of Omar Khayyám* later, but ends of lines and verses were part of the culture I grew up in, so that when I read the whole poem I recognized large parts of it, rather than meeting it for the first time:

> There was a Door to which I found no Key:
> There was a Veil past which I could not see:
> Some little talk awhile of ME and THEE
> There seem'd—and then no more of THEE and ME.

When I was a student Victorian poetry was unfashionable and even despised. Browning and Tennyson, T. S. Eliot famously said, were poets and they thought, but "did not feel their thoughts as immediately as the odour of a rose." Rhyme and rhythm were out of fashion too—Pound had taught us to "break the pentameter." I think I knew even then that Eliot was haunted by both Tennyson and Browning, as it was clear that Pound had learned his craft from Browning. I did not think the great Victorians were any less intelligent—or any less passionate—than the great moderns. Now we are far enough from them to be able to read them anew and without prejudice—and we have lived through free verse and its subtleties long enough to be able to meet the despised pentameter with a new shock of excitement. Tennyson and Browning have been re-assessed. And FitzGerald has perhaps become unfamiliar—so that the particular note of his lyric irony, his passionate scepticism can startle us again.

The *Rubáiyát* embodies the meeting of two very different men, from widely separated times, artistic traditions, and cultures. Omar Khayyám was born on May 18, 1048, in northeast Persia—the date was established in 1941, on the basis of an early horoscope. Edward FitzGerald was born on March 31, 1809, in a country house in Suffolk. Khayyám was a famous mathematician and astronomer, a follower of Avicenna. FitzGerald was the rich son of a society beauty, a Cambridge friend of Tennyson and the Apostles, whose chosen lifestyle became a somewhat spartan reclusiveness in Suffolk, where he cared for his garden and roamed the beaches making friends with local boatmen. FitzGerald married late in life—he was forty-seven and his bride was forty-eight—and the marriage was a disaster from the beginning. FitzGerald did not live with his wife for very long, but work was begun on his translation of the *Rubáiyát* in the early unhappy days of his marriage when he had escaped to the family home of his friend William Browne. He had learned Persian four years earlier to work with Edward Cowell, an orientalist, who transcribed the manuscript from which FitzGerald first read Khayyám. Now in hiding from his new bride he wrote that he had "put away almost all Books except Omar Khayyám!, which I could not help looking over in a Paddock covered with Buttercups and brushed by a delicious Breeze, while a dainty racing Filly of W. Browne's came startling up to wonder and snuff about me." "Omar," he wrote "breathes a sort of Consolation to me!" His "sort of Epicurean Eclogue in a Persian Garden" began in a paddock of English buttercups—and, as has often been pointed out, the idea of a garden was introduced into Omar's poems by FitzGerald himself.

The *rubái* (*rubáiyát* is the plural) is a two-line stanza of Persian poetry, divided further into two, of which the first, second, and last parts must rhyme, a pattern that FitzGerald reproduced, with his unrhymed third line in his quatrains. Persian *rubáiyát* are separate epigrammatic, witty, or reflective stanzas, and collections were originally arranged alphabetically, according to the last letter of the rhyme. Omar Khayyám was not particularly famous for his poetry— he wrote it as civilised Japanese wrote haiku, and the *rubáiyát* were a favoured form amongst Persian intellectuals, freethinkers, philosophers opposed to religious orthodoxy and fanaticism. Many *rubáiyát* in many manuscripts are ascribed to Khayyám, and the ascriptions are argued over. FitzGerald started work on a manuscript that contained 158 poems—Cowell later found a manuscript in Calcutta with 516 poems, and in J. B. Nicolas's French translation, which appeared whilst FitzGerald was preparing his second edition, there were 464 more. Khayyám is a voice that speaks briefly—sharply, wittily, sadly—through a multitude of precise stanzas. FitzGerald's response to Khayyám's mixture of the "Grave" and the "Gay" gave rise to an English poem that changed the landscape of English poetry and added a new tone of voice to the English lyric.

FitzGerald did not claim to be a painstaking, scholarly translator. He created his own poem out of his sympathy for what he felt was the moral and emotional power of the Persian's belief in the pleasure of the moment, the transitoriness of life, the energetic rejection of religious consolation. He had, he said, transfused the poem with his own disposition. "I suppose very few People have ever taken such pains in Translation as I have, though certainly not to be literal. But at all Cost, a Thing must *live*: with a transfusion of one's own worse Life if one can't retain the Original's better. Better a live Sparrow than a stuffed Eagle."

Something in the fusion of hedonism and melancholy FitzGerald created has gripped the imaginations of both the Victorians and subsequent generations. At first it seemed as though this might not be so. The book was published in 1859—the year of Darwin's *Origin of Species*—two hundred and fifty copies, with no author named. By 1861 few had been sold, and the remainder, reduced from a shilling to a penny, were put into the bargain box of a bookshop. There they were found by a young scholar, who gave copies to his friends, including Richard Monckton Milnes, Richard Burton, and Dante Gabriel Rossetti. Rossetti bought copies for Swinburne and Browning. Swinburne gave copies to Burne-Jones and William Morris, and one made its way to Ruskin, who wrote to the anonymous author, "I never did—till this day—read anything so glorious, to my mind, as this poem . . ." Charles Eliot Norton, at Harvard, launched the poem on its immense popularity in the United States, and discovered the identity of the author.

Why was it so successful?

Part of the reason may be to do with the passion for the Orient in nineteenth-century England. Burton, who translated the *Arabian Nights* and added a great deal of bizarre eroticism of his own, and also Monckton Milnes, associated the Orient with sensuality, freedom from restraint, and mystery. More subtly, perhaps, poets like Tennyson were interested in "Persian poetry" and the traditions of the *ghazal*, in which human emotions are expressed through the flowers, the cypresses, and the nightingales in Eastern gardens. In Tennyson's early "Recollections of the *Arabian Nights*"—

> The living airs of middle night
> Died round the bulbul as he sung;
> Not he: but something which possessed
> The darkness of the world, delight,
> Life, anguish, death, immortal love . . .

—a Persian nightingale sings like Keats's English one. Lady Tennyson is said to have prevented Tennyson from learning Persian, hiding his texts because she feared for his eyesight and encouraging badminton as a safer activity. But some of his greatest love lyrics are "Persian":

> Now sleeps the crimson petal, now the white;
> Now waves the cypress in the palace walk;
> Now winks the gold fin in the porphyry font:
> The firefly wakens; waken thou with me.

Maud could not be more English, set in a "high Hall garden" with English birds and daffodils, but that poem too is suffused with Persian feeling—Maud's harsh brother is referred to as a "Sultan," the cedars of her lawn weep for Lebanon, and in "Come into the garden, Maud," Tennyson personifies the red rose and the white, passion and fear, in a way that fuses English rose and oriental sensuality. Tennyson's greatest poems, like FitzGerald's *Rubáiyát*, are constructed of a series of lyrics, changing moods, and rhythmically condensed thoughts and feelings. *Maud* is a case in point. *In Memoriam*, one of the greatest poems in the English language, works its thought on death through the closed quatrains, the memorable epigrams, the *song*, as *The Rubáiyát of Omar Khayyám* does.

The mood and meaning of the poems—both Khayyám's and FitzGerald's—have caused dispute. Khayyám has been claimed as a Sufic mystic, using hidden motifs and symbols to express a love for a God the Creator. In this tradition the imagery of men and women as pots made, broken, and remade, of flowers springing from dead earth, can be seen as an expression of the creation as the continuing work and manifestation of God. The Biblical *Song of Songs* uses erotic imagery as a metaphor for divine love, and FitzGerald's friend Cowell, who introduced him to Khayyám, was a devout Christian, and argued passionately with FitzGerald that the *Rubáiyát* also concealed religious mysticism. Khayyám himself lived at the time of a religious revival under the Seljuk sultans and had to be circumspect about his views. The fact that he was attacked shortly after his death both by scholastic Muslims and by a Sufic mystic suggests that he had a reputation as a materialist and empiricist; wine is forbidden to Islamic believers, so his praise of drinking is at least on the surface blasphemous. It is certain that FitzGerald believed that Khayyám, like himself, was an unbeliever, who expressed the sense that this life is all, and is fleeting. He defended his "Infidel and Epicurean" alter ego against his religious friends.

It is interesting that Browning, in "Rabbi ben Ezra," another reflective poem about a Middle Eastern sage, composed in tight stanzas, used Khayyám/FitzGerald's "eastern" metaphor of pot and potter to attack the poem.

> . . . All I could never be,
> All, men ignored in me,
> This, I was worth to God, whose wheel the
>   pitcher shaped.

> Ay, note that Potter's wheel,
> That metaphor! and feel
> Why time spins fast, why passive lies our clay,—
> Thou, to whom fools propound,
> When the wine makes its round,
> "Since life fleets, all is change; the Past gone,
>   seize today!"

> Fool! All that is, at all,
> Lasts ever, past recall;
> Earth changes, but thy soul and God stand sure: . . .

Browning may have thought FitzGerald and Khayyám were fools, but their ideas provoked a widespread enthusiastic response. Partly this appealed to the mood of "decadence," of Swinburne's contempt for the "pale Galilean" whose breath made the world grey, of his opposition of the "lilies and languors of virtue" to the "raptures and roses of vice." But the poem appealed too to the deep uncertainties about the nature of life on earth aroused by the discoveries of Darwin and the speculations of the geologists about vanished species. Nietzsche's cry for a "strong pessimism," his delight in the Dionysiac dance and drunkenness, are part of the same complex movement, along with George Eliot's serious observation of the ordered and unresponsive heavens. Tennyson's doubt was more eloquent than his faith, and had the strongest tunes. His *Vision of Sin*, published in 1842, has rhythms and themes that prefigure FitzGerald.

> "Fill the cup and fill the can:
> Have a rouse before the morn:
> Every moment dies a man,
> Every moment one is born . . .
>
> "Fill the can and fill the cup:
> All the windy ways of men
> Are but dust that rises up,
> And is lightly laid again."

The glory of FitzGerald's poem is the strength of the writing. It is at once rich and strange, and familiar with the whole culture into which it entered, with its deliberate echoes of the Bible and of Shakespeare. The motifs of the *Rubáiyát*—Khayyám's own and FitzGerald's additions, including the unifying metaphor of the garden—are old, and therefore powerful and moving. The *Rubáiyát*'s pessimism is Hamlet's:

> Imperial Caesar, dead and turned to clay,
> Might stop a hole to keep the wind away.

It recalls a wonderful image, recorded by the Venerable Bede:

> "Such," he said, "O King, seems to me the present life of men on earth, in comparison with that time which to us is uncertain, as if when on a winter's night you sit feasting with your ealdormen and thegns,—a single sparrow should fly swiftly into the hall, and coming in at one door, instantly fly out through another. In that time when it is indoors, it is not touched by the fury of winter, but yet, this smallest space of calmness

being passed, almost in a flash, from winter going
into winter again, it is lost to your eyes."

This, in a northern king's hall, is a wintry image of transitori-
ness, related to the battered caravanserai of the Sultans, whose doors
are alternate Night and Day. Or we can hear in FitzGerald's *Rubáiyát*
the sardonic voice of the writer of the Book of Ecclesiastes:

> "What profit hath a man of all his labour
> which he taketh under the sun?
> One generation passeth away, and another
> generation cometh; but the earth abideth forever.
> The sun also ariseth, and the sun goeth
> down, and hasteth to his place where he arose."
> (1:3-5)
> "Then I commended mirth, because a man
> hath no better thing under the sun, than to eat,
> and to drink, and to be merry: for that shall abide
> with him of his labour the days of his life, which
> God giveth him under the sun." (2:24)

FitzGerald's verse is insidiously memorable. It sings in the mind,
controlled by its steady rapid rhythm and its strong, emphatic, reit-
erated rhyme, which in turn is made mysteriously open by the one
unrhymed line in each verse. Our hearts beat five times for each of
our breaths, and the iambic pentameter FitzGerald used is the
rhythm of our passing lives themselves. Generations of readers have
known his poem "by heart"—the six long columns of quotations
from it in *The Oxford Dictionary of Quotations* make a long poem in
themselves. FitzGerald's *Rubáiyát* still has the power to become part
of and change its readers as Khayyám became part of and changed
FitzGerald.

—A. S. Byatt
London, 1996

LIST OF ILLUSTRATIONS

FIRST EDITION

I.

Page

Awake! for Morning in the Bowl of Night
Has flung the Stone that puts the Stars to Flight
And Lo! the Hunter of the East has caught
The Sultán's Turret in a Noose of Light

1

XI.

Here with a Loaf of Bread beneath the Bough,
A Flask of Wine, a Book of Verse—and Thou
Beside me singing in the Wilderness—
And Wilderness is Paradise enow

16

XIII.

Look to the Rose that blows about us—"Lo,
Laughing," she says, "into the World I blow:
At once the silken Tassel of my Purse
Tear, and its Treasure on the Garden throw"

32

OMAR KHAYYÁM

XXIV.
Page

Alike for those who for To-day prepare,
And those that after a To-morrow stare,
  A Muezzîn from the Tower of Darkness cries
" Fools ! your Reward is neither Here nor There !"   48

XLII.

And lately, by the Tavern Door agape,
Came stealing through the Dusk an Angel Shape
  Bearing a Vessel on his Shoulder; and
He bid me taste of it; and 'twas—the Grape !   64

LXXII.

Alas, that Spring should vanish with the Rose !
That Youth's sweet-scented Manuscript should close !
  The Nightingale that in the Branches sang,
Ah, whence, and whither flown again, who knows !   72

LIST OF ILLUSTRATIONS

SECOND EDITION

XI.

Page

With me along the Strip of Herbage strown
That just divides the desert from the sown,
    Where name of Slave and Sultân is forgot—
And Peace to Máhmúd on his golden Throne?   96

XX.

The Palace that to Heav'n his pillars threw,
And Kings the forehead on his threshold drew—
    I saw the solitary Ringdove there,
And "Coo, coo, coo," she cried; and "Coo, coo, coo" 112

XL.

For I remember stopping by the way
To watch a Potter thumping his wet Clay:
    And with its all-obliterated Tongue
It murmur'd—"Gently, Brother, gently, pray!"   128

XLIV.

Do you, within your little hour of Grace,
The waving Cypress in your Arms enlace,
    Before the Mother back into her arms
Fold, and dissolve you in a last embrace   144

OMAR KHAYYÁM

LV.

Page

Oh, plagued no more with Human or Divine,
To-morrow's tangle to itself resign,
    And lose your fingers in the tresses of
The Cypress-slender Minister of Wine   160

LXXII.

Heav'n but the Vision of fulfill'd Desire,
And Hell the Shadow of a Soul on fire,
    Cast on the Darkness into which Ourselves,
So late emerged from, shall so soon expire   176

RUBÁIYÁT

OF

OMAR KHAYYÁM OF NAISHÁPÚR

THE FIRST EDITION
OF THE TRANSLATION

OMAR KHAYYÁM

I

Awake! for Morning in the Bowl of Night
Has flung the Stone that puts the Stars
    to Flight:
  And Lo! the Hunter of the East has
    caught
The Sultán's Turret in a Noose of Light.

II

Dreaming when Dawn's Left Hand was in
    the Sky
I heard a Voice within the Tavern cry,
  "Awake, my Little ones, and fill the
    Cup
Before Life's Liquor in its Cup be dry."

OMAR KHAYYÁM

III

And, as the Cock crew, those who stood
before
The Tavern shouted—"Open then the
Door!
You know how little while we have to
stay,
And, once departed, may return no more."

IV

Now the New Year reviving old Desires,
The thoughtful Soul to Solitude retires,
Where the WHITE HAND OF MOSES on
the Bough
Puts out, and Jesus from the Ground
suspires.

OMAR KHAYYÁM

V

Irám indeed is gone with all its Rose,
And Jamshýd's Sev'n-ring'd Cup where no
    one knows ;
    But still the Vine her ancient Ruby
    yields,
And still a Garden by the Water blows.

VI

And David's Lips are lock't ; but in divine
High piping Pehleví, with " Wine ! Wine !
    Wine !
    Red Wine ! "—the Nightingale cries to
    the Rose
That yellow Cheek of hers to incarnadine.

OMAR KHAYYÁM

VII

Come, fill the Cup, and in the Fire of
    Spring
The Winter Garment of Repentance fling:
    The Bird of Time has but a little way
To fly—and Lo! the Bird is on the Wing.

VIII

And look—a thousand Blossoms with the
    Day
Woke—and a thousand scatter'd into
    Clay:
    And this first Summer Month that
      brings the Rose
Shall take Jamshýd and Kaikobád away.

OMAR KHAYYÁM

IX

But come with old Khayyám, and leave
    the Lot
Of Kaikobád and Kaikhosrú forgot:
    Let Rustum lay about him as he will,
Or Hátim Tai cry Supper—heed them not.

X

With me along some Strip of Herbage
    strown
That just divides the desert from the
    sown,
    Where name of Slave and Sultán scarce
    is known,
And pity Sultán Máhmúd on his Throne.

OMAR KHAYYÁM

XI

Here with a Loaf of Bread beneath the
    Bough,
A Flask of Wine, a Book of Verse—and
    Thou
  Beside me singing in the Wilderness—
And Wilderness is Paradise enow.

XII

"How sweet is mortal Sovranty!"—think
    some:
Others—"How blest the Paradise to
    come!"
  Ah, take the Cash in hand and waive
    the Rest;
Oh, the brave Music of a *distant* Drum!

XIII

Look to the Rose that blows about us—
"Lo,
Laughing," she says, "into the World I
blow:
At once the silken Tassel of my Purse
Tear, and its Treasure on the Garden
throw."

XIV

The Worldly Hope men set their Hearts
upon
Turns Ashes—or it prospers; and anon,
Like Snow upon the Desert's dusty Face
Lighting a little Hour or two—is gone.

OMAR KHAYYÁM

XV

And those who husbanded the Golden
    Grain,
And those who flung it to the Winds like
    Rain,
    Alike to no such aureate Earth are turn'd
As, buried once, Men want dug up again.

XVI

Think, in this batter'd Caravanserai
Whose Doorways are alternate Night and
    Day,
    How Sultán after Sultán with his Pomp
Abode his Hour or two, and went his way.

OMAR KHAYYÁM

XVII

They say the Lion and the Lizard keep
The Courts where Jamshýd gloried and
drank deep;
And Bahrám, that great Hunter—the
Wild Ass
Stamps o'er his Head, and he lies fast
asleep.

XVIII

I sometimes think that never blows so red
The Rose as where some buried Cæsar
bled;
That every Hyacinth the Garden wears
Dropt in its Lap from some once lovely
Head.

OMAR KHAYYÁM

XIX

And this delightful Herb whose tender
    Green
Fledges the River's Lip on which we lean—
    Ah, lean upon it lightly! for who knows
From what once lovely Lip it springs un-
    seen!

XX

Ah, my Belovéd, fill the Cup that clears
To-day of past Regrets and future Fears—
    To-morrow?—Why, To-morrow I may be
Myself with Yesterday's Sev'n Thousand
    Years.

XXI

Lo! some we loved, the loveliest and the
    best
That Time and Fate of all their Vintage
    prest,
   Have drunk their Cup a Round or two
     before,
And one by one crept silently to Rest.

XXII

And we, that now make merry in the Room
They left, and Summer dresses in new
    Bloom,
   Ourselves must we beneath the Couch
     of Earth
Descend, ourselves to make a Couch—for
    whom?

OMAR KHAYYÁM

XXIII

Ah, make the most of what we yet may
    spend,
Before we too into the Dust descend ;
   Dust into Dust, and under Dust, to lie,
Sans Wine, sans Song, sans Singer, and
    —sans End.

XXIV

Alike for those who for To-day prepare,
And those that after a To-morrow stare,
   A Muezzín from the Tower of Darkness
    cries
"Fools ! your Reward is neither Here nor
   There !"

OMAR KHAYYÁM

XXV

Why, all the Saints and Sages who
    discuss'd
Of the Two Worlds so learnedly, are thrust
    Like foolish Prophets forth ; their Words
    to Scorn
Are scatter'd, and their Mouths are stopt
    with Dust.

XXVI

Oh, come with old Khayyám, and leave
    the Wise
To talk ; one thing is certain, that Life
    flies ;
    One thing is certain, and the Rest is
    Lies ;
The Flower that once has blown for ever
    dies.

OMAR KHAYYÁM

XXVII

Myself when young did eagerly frequent
Doctor and Saint, and heard great Argu-
    ment
About it and about: but evermore
Came out by the same Door as in I went.

XXVIII

With them the Seed of Wisdom did I sow,
And with my own hand labour'd it to grow:
And this was all the Harvest that I
    reap'd—
"I came like Water, and like Wind I go."

OMAR KHAYYÁM

XXIX

Into this Universe, and *why* not knowing,
Nor *whence*, like Water willy-nilly flowing:
  And out of it, as Wind along the Waste,
I know not *whither*, willy-nilly blowing.

XXX

What, without asking, hither hurried
    whence ?
And, without asking, *whither* hurried hence !
  Another and another Cup to drown
The Memory of this Impertinence !

OMAR KHAYYÁM

XXXI

Up from Earth's Centre through the
    Seventh Gate
I rose, and on the Throne of Saturn sate,
  And many Knots unravel'd by the Road;
But not the Knot of Human Death and
    Fate.

XXXII

There was a Door to which I found no
    Key:
There was a Veil past which I could not
    see:
  Some little Talk awhile of ME and THEE
There seem'd—and then no more of THEE
    and ME.

OMAR KHAYYÁM

XXXIII

Then to the rolling Heav'n itself I cried,
Asking, "What Lamp had Destiny to
    guide
  Her little Children stumbling in the
    Dark ? "
And—"A blind Understanding !" Heav'n
replied.

XXXIV

Then to this earthen Bowl did I adjourn
My Lip the secret Well of Life to learn :
  And Lip to Lip it murmur'd—"While
    you live
Drink !—for once dead you never shall
return."

OMAR KHAYYÁM

XXXV

I think the Vessel, that with fugitive
Articulation answer'd, once did live,
    And merry-make; and the cold Lip I
      kiss'd
How many Kisses might it take—and
      give !

XXXVI

For in the Market-place, one Dusk of Day,
I watch'd the Potter thumping his wet
      Clay :
    And with its all obliterated Tongue
It murmur'd—" Gently, Brother, gently,
      pray ! "

OMAR KHAYYÁM

XXXVII

Ah, fill the Cup :—what boots it to repeat
How Time is slipping underneath our
    Feet :
Unborn To-morrow, and dead Yesterday
Why fret about them if To-day be sweet!

XXXVIII

One Moment in Annihilation's Waste,
One Moment, of the Well of Life to
    taste—
The Stars are setting and the Caravan
Starts for the Dawn of Nothing—Oh, make
    haste!

XXXIX

How long, how long, in definite Pursuit
Of This and That endeavour and dispute?
  Better be merry with the fruitful Grape
Than sadder after none, or bitter, Fruit.

XL

You know, my Friends, how long since in
      my House
For a new Marriage I did make Carouse:
  Divorced old barren Reason from my
      Bed,
And took the Daughter of the Vine to
      Spouse.

OMAR KHAYYÁM

XLI

For "Is" and "Is-not" though *with* Rule
    and Line
And "Up-and-down" *without*, I could define,
    I yet in all I only cared to know,
Was never deep in anything but—Wine.

XLII

And lately, by the Tavern Door agape,
Came stealing through the Dusk an Angel
    Shape
    Bearing a Vessel on his Shoulder; and
He bid me taste of it; and 'twas—the
    Grape!

OMAR KHAYYÁM

XLIII

The Grape that can with Logic absolute
The Two-and-Seventy jarring Sects con-
    fute :
The subtle Alchemist that in a Trice
Life's leaden Metal into Gold transmute.

XLIV

The mighty Mahmúd, the victorious Lord,
That all the misbelieving and black Horde
    Of Fears and Sorrows that infest the
    Soul
Scatters and slays with his enchanted
    Sword.

45

XLV

But leave the Wise to wrangle, and with
    me
The Quarrel of the Universe let be :
  And, in some corner of the Hubbub
    coucht,
Make Game of that which makes as much
    of Thee.

XLVI

For in and out, above, about, below,
'Tis nothing but a Magic Shadow-show
  Play'd in a Box whose Candle is the
    Sun,
Round which we Phantom Figures come
    and go.

OMAR KHAYYÁM

XLVII

And if the Wine you drink, the Lip you
  press,
End in the Nothing all Things end in—
  Yes—
  Then fancy while Thou art, Thou art
    but what
Thou shalt be—Nothing—Thou shalt not
  be less.

XLVIII

While the Rose blows along the River
  Brink,
With old Khayyám the Ruby Vintage drink:
  And when the Angel with his darker
    Draught
Draws up to Thee—take that, and do not
  shrink.

OMAR KHAYYÁM

XLIX

'Tis all a Chequer-board of Nights and
    Days
Where Destiny with Men for Pieces plays:
  Hither and thither moves, and mates,
    and slays,
And one by one back in the Closet lays.

L

 The Ball no Question makes of Ayes and
    Noes,
But Right or Left as strikes the Player
    goes ;
  And He that toss'd Thee down into the
    Field,
He knows about it all—HE knows—HE
    knows !

LI

The Moving Finger writes; and, having
  writ,
Moves on: nor all thy Piety nor Wit
  Shall lure it back to cancel half a Line,
Nor all thy Tears wash out a Word of it.

LII

And that inverted Bowl we call The Sky,
Whereunder crawling coop't we live and
  die,
  Lift not thy hands to *It* for help—for It
Rolls impotently on as Thou or I.

OMAR KHAYYÁM

LIII

With Earth's first Clay They did the Last
    Man's knead,
And then of the Last Harvest sow'd the
    Seed:
  Yea, the first Morning of Creation wrote
What the Last Dawn of Reckoning shall
    read.

LIV

I tell Thee this—When, starting from the
    Goal,
Over the shoulders of the flaming Foal
  Of Heav'n Parwín and Mushtara they
    flung,
In my predestined Plot of Dust and Soul

LV

The Vine had struck a Fibre ; which about
If clings my Being—let the Súfi flout ;
  Of my Base Metal may be filed a Key,
That shall unlock the Door he howls
    without.

LVI

And this I know : whether the one True
    Light,
Kindle to Love, or Wrath consume me
    quite,
  One glimpse of It within the Tavern
    caught
Better than in the Temple lost outright.

OMAR KHAYYÁM

LVII

Oh, Thou, who didst with Pitfall and with
    Gin
Beset the Road I was to wander in,
  Thou wilt not with Predestination round
Enmesh me, and impute my Fall to Sin?

LVIII

Oh, Thou, who Man of baser Earth didst
    make,
And who with Eden didst devise the
    Snake;
  For all the Sin wherewith the Face of
    Man
Is blacken'd, Man's Forgiveness give—
    and take!

    *   *   *   *   *

KÚZA-NÁMA

LIX

Listen again. One evening at the Close
Of Ramazán, ere the better Moon arose,
  In that old Potter's Shop I stood alone
With the clay Population round in Rows.

LX

And, strange to tell, among the Earthen
    Lot
Some could articulate, while others not :
  And suddenly one more impatient cried—
"Who *is* the Potter, pray, and who the
    Pot ?"

OMAR KHAYYÁM

LXI

Then said another—"Surely not in vain
My Substance from the common Earth
  was ta'en,
 That He who subtly wrought me into
  Shape
Should stamp me back to common Earth
  again."

LXII

Another said—"Why, ne'er a peevish Boy,
Would break the Bowl from which he
  drank in Joy;
Shall He that *made* the Vessel in pure Love
And Fancy, in an after Rage destroy!"

LXIII

None answer'd this ; but after Silence
    spake
A Vessel of a more ungainly Make :
   "They sneer at me for leaning all awry ;
What ! did the Hand then of the Potter
    shake ? "

LXIV

Said one—" Folks of a surly Tapster tell,
And daub his Visage with the Smoke of
    Hell ;
   They talk of some strict Testing of us—
    Pish !
He's a Good Fellow, and 'twill all be well."

LXV

Then said another with a long-drawn Sigh,
"My Clay with long oblivion is gone dry :
But, fill me with the old familiar Juice,
Methinks I might recover by-and-bye !"

LXVI

So while the Vessels one by one were
    speaking,
One spied the little Crescent all were
    seeking :
And then they jogg'd each other,
    "Brother, Brother !
Hark to the Porter's Shoulder-knot a
    creaking !"

      *   *   *   *   *

OMAR KHAYYÁM

LXVII

Ah, with the Grape my fading Life provide,
And wash my Body whence the Life has
    died,
    And in a Windingsheet of Vine-leaf
    wrapt,
So bury me by some sweet Garden-side.

LXVIII

That ev'n my buried Ashes such a Snare
Of Perfume shall fling up into the Air,
    As not a True Believer passing by
But shall be overtaken unaware.

OMAR KHAYYÁM

LXIX

Indeed the Idols I have loved so long
Have done my Credit in Men's Eye much
    wrong:
  Have drown'd my Honour in a shallow
    Cup,
And sold my Reputation for a Song.

LXX

Indeed, indeed, Repentance oft before
I swore—but was I sober when I swore?
  And then and then came Spring, and
    Rose-in-hand
My thread-bare Penitence apieces tore.

OMAR KHAYYÁM

LXXI

And much as Wine has play'd the Infidel,
And robb'd me of my Robe of Honour—
    well,
  I often wonder what the Vintners buy
One half so precious as the Goods they
    sell.

LXXII

Alas, that Spring should vanish with the
    Rose!
That Youth's sweet-scented Manuscript
    should close!
  The Nightingale that in the Branches
    sang,
Ah, whence, and whither flown again, who
    knows!

OMAR KHAYYÁM

LXXIII

Ah Love! could thou and I with Fate
    conspire
To grasp this sorry Scheme of Things
    entire,
    Would not we shatter it to bits—and
    then
Re-mould it nearer to the Heart's Desire!

LXXIV

Ah, Moon of my Delight who know'st no
    wane,
The Moon of Heav'n is rising once again:
    How oft hereafter rising shall she look
Through this same Garden after me—in
    vain!

OMAR KHAYYÁM

LXXV

And when Thyself with shining Foot shall
pass
Among the Guests Star-scatter'd on the
Grass,
And in thy joyous Errand reach the
Spot
Where I made one—turn down an empty
Glass !

TAMÁM SHUD

RUBÁIYÁT

OF

OMAR KHAYYÁM OF NAISHÁPÚR

THE SECOND EDITION
OF THE TRANSLATION

OMAR KHAYYÁM

I

Wake! For the Sun behind yon Eastern
 height
Has chased the Session of the Stars from
 Night;
 And, to the field of Heav'n ascending,
 strikes
The Sultán's Turret with a Shaft of Light.

II

Before the phantom of False morning died,
Methought a Voice within the Tavern
 cried,
 "When all the Temple is prepared
 within,
Why lags the drowsy Worshipper out-
 side?"

OMAR KHAYYÁM

III

And, as the Cock crew, those who stood
    before
The Tavern shouted—"Open then the
    Door!
  You know how little while we have to
    stay,
And, once departed, may return no more."

IV

Now the New Year reviving old Desires,
The thoughtful Soul to Solitude retires,
  Where the WHITE HAND OF MOSES on
    the Bough
Puts out, and Jesus from the Ground
    suspires.

OMAR KHAYYÁM

V

Iram indeed is gone with all his Rose,
And Jamshýd's Sev'n-ring'd Cup where no
    one knows ;
But still a Ruby gushes from the Vine,
And many a Garden by the Water blows.

VI

And David's lips are lockt ; but in divine
High-piping Péhleví, with "Wine ! Wine !
    Wine !
    Red Wine !"—the Nightingale cries to
    the Rose
That sallow cheek of hers to incarnadine.

OMAR KHAYYÁM

VII

Come, fill the Cup, and in the fire of Spring
Your Winter-garment of Repentance fling :
    The Bird of Time has but a little way
To flutter—and the Bird is on the Wing.

VIII

Whether at Naishápúr or Babylon,
Whether the Cup with sweet or bitter run,
    The Wine of Life keeps oozing drop by
        drop,
The Leaves of Life keep falling one by one.

OMAR KHAYYÁM

IX

Morning a thousand Roses brings, you
    say;
Yes, but where leaves the Rose of Yester-
    day?
  And this first Summer month that brings
    the Rose
Shall take Jamshýd and Kaikobád away.

X

Well, let it take them! What have we to
    do
With Kaikobád the Great, or Kaikhosrú?
  Let Rustum cry "To Battle!" as he
    likes,
Or Hátim Tai "To Supper"—heed not you.

OMAR KHAYYÁM

XI

With me along the Strip of Herbage
    strown
That just divides the desert from the sown,
    Where name of Slave and Sultán is
      forgot—
And Peace to Máhmúd on his golden
    Throne?

XII

Here with a little Bread beneath the
    Bough,
A Flask of Wine, a Book of Verse—and
    Thou
    Beside me singing in the Wilderness—
Oh, Wilderness were Paradise enow!

OMAR KHAYYÁM

XIII

Some for the Glories of This World ; and
    some
Sigh for the Prophet's Paradise to come ;
  Ah, take the Cash, and let the promise
    go,
Nor heed the music of a distant Drum !

XIV

Were it not Folly, Spider-like to spin
The Thread of present Life away to win—
  What ? for ourselves, who know not if
    we shall
Breathe out the very Breath we now
    breathe in !

OMAR KHAYYÁM

XV

Look to the blowing Rose about us—" Lo,
Laughing," she says, "into the world I
    blow :
At once the silken tassel of my Purse
Tear, and its Treasure on the Garden
    throw."

XVI

For those who husbanded the Golden grain,
And those who flung it to the winds like
    Rain,
    Alike to no such aureate Earth are
    turn'd
As, buried once, Men want dug up again.

OMAR KHAYYÁM

XVII

The Worldly Hope men set their Hearts
 upon
Turns Ashes—or it prospers; and anon,
 Like Snow upon the Desert's dusty Face,
Lighting a little hour or two—was gone.

XVIII

Think, in this batter'd Caravanserai
Whose Portals are alternate Night and
 Day,
 How Sultán after Sultán with his Pomp
Abode his destined Hour, and went his
 way.

OMAR KHAYYÁM

XIX

They say the Lion and the Lizard keep
The Courts where Jamshýd gloried and
    drank deep :
And Bahrám, that great Hunter—the
    Wild Ass
Stamps o'er his Head, but cannot break
    his Sleep.

XX

The Palace that to Heav'n his pillars
    threw,
And Kings the forehead on his threshold
    drew—
I saw the solitary Ringdove there,
And "Coo, coo, coo," she cried; and
"Coo, coo, coo."

OMAR KHAYYÁM

XXI

Ah, my Belovéd, fill the Cup that clears
To-DAY of past Regret and Future Fears :
  To-morrow !—Why, To-morrow I may be
Myself with Yesterday's Sev'n thousand
  Years.

XXII

For some we loved, the loveliest and the
  best
That from his Vintage rolling Time has
  prest,
  Have drunk their Cup a Round or two
  before,
And one by one crept silently to rest.

OMAR KHAYYÁM

XXIII

And we, that now make merry in the Room
They left, and Summer dresses in new
bloom,
Ourselves must we beneath the Couch
of Earth
Descend—ourselves to make a Couch—
for whom?

XXIV

I sometimes think that never blows so red
The Rose as where some buried Cæsar
bled;
That every Hyacinth the Garden wears
Dropt in her Lap from some once lovely
Head.

OMAR KHAYYÁM

XXV

And this delightful Herb whose living
    Green
Fledges the River's Lip on which we lean—
    Ah, lean upon it lightly! for who knows
From what once lovely Lip it springs
    unseen!

XXVI

Ah, make the most of what we yet may
    spend,
Before we too into the Dust descend;
    Dust into Dust, and under Dust, to lie,
Sans Wine, sans Song, sans Singer, and
    —sans End!

OMAR KHAYYÁM

XXVII

Alike for those who for To-day prepare,
And those that after some To-morrow
stare,
    A Muezzín from the Tower of Darkness
cries,
"Fools! your Reward is neither Here nor
There."

XXVIII

Another Voice, when I am sleeping, cries,
"The Flower should open with the Morn-
ing skies."
    And a retreating Whisper, as I wake—
"The Flower that once has blown for
ever dies."

107

OMAR KHAYYÁM

XXIX

Why, all the Saints and Sages who
    discuss'd
Of the Two Worlds so learnedly, are
    thrust
  Like foolish Prophets forth; their
    Words to Scorn
Are scatter'd, and their Mouths are stopt
    with Dust.

XXX

Myself when young did eagerly frequent
Doctor and Saint, and heard great
    argument
  About it and about: but evermore
Came out by the same door as in I went.

OMAR KHAYYÁM

XXXI

With them the seed of Wisdom did I sow,
And with my own hand wrought to make
    it grow;
    And this was all the Harvest that I
        reap'd—
"I came like Water, and like Wind I go."

XXXII

Into this Universe, and *Why* not knowing,
Nor *Whence*, like Water willy-nilly flowing;
    And out of it, as Wind along the Waste,
I know not *Whither*, willy-nilly blowing.

OMAR KHAYYÁM

XXXIII

What, without asking, hither hurried
    Whence?
And, without asking, *Whither* hurried hence!
  Ah! contrite Heav'n endowed us with
      the Vine
To drug the memory of that insolence!

XXXIV

Up from Earth's Centre through the
      Seventh Gate
I rose, and on the Throne of Saturn sate;
  And many Knots unravel'd by the Road;
But not the Master-knot of Human Fate.

OMAR KHAYYÁM

XXXV

There was the Door to which I found no
    Key:
There was the Veil through which I could
    not see:
  Some little talk awhile of ME and THEE
There was—and then no more of THEE
    and ME.

XXXVI

Earth could not answer: nor the Seas
    that mourn
In flowing Purple, of their Lord forlorn;
  Nor Heaven, with those eternal Signs
    reveal'd
And hidden by the sleeve of Night and
    Morn.

OMAR KHAYYÁM

XXXVII

Then of the THEE IN ME who works behind
The Veil of Universe I cried to find
    A Lamp to guide me through the Dark-
      ness ; and
Something then said—" An Understanding
    blind."

XXXVIII

Then to the Lip of this poor earthen Urn
I lean'd, the Secret Well of Life to learn :
    And Lip to Lip it murmur'd—" While
      you live,
Drink !—for, once dead, you never shall
    return."

OMAR KHAYYÁM

XXXIX

I think the Vessel, that with fugitive
Articulation answer'd, once did live,
 And drink; and that impassive Lip I
  kiss'd,
How many Kisses might it take—and
  give!

XL

For I remember stopping by the way
To watch a Potter thumping his wet Clay:
 And with its all-obliterated Tongue
It murmur'd—" Gently, Brother, gently,
  pray!"

OMAR KHAYYÁM

XLI

For has not such a Story from of Old
Down Man's successive generations roll'd
  Of such a clod of saturated Earth
Cast by the Maker into Human mould?

XLII

And not a drop that from our Cups we
    throw
On the parcht herbage but may steal below
  To quench the fire of Anguish in some
    Eye
There hidden—far beneath, and long ago.

OMAR KHAYYÁM

XLIII

As then the Tulip for her wonted sup
Of Heavenly Vintage lifts her chalice up,
   Do you, twin offspring of the soil, till
      Heav'n
To Earth invert you like an empty Cup.

XLIV

Do you, within your little hour of Grace,
The waving Cypress in your Arms enlace,
   Before the Mother back into her arms
Fold, and dissolve you in a last embrace.

OMAR KHAYYÁM

XLV

And if the Cup you drink, the Lip you
    press,
End in what All begins and ends in—Yes;
    Imagine then you *are* what heretofore
You *were*—hereafter you shall not be less.

XLVI

So when at last the Angel of the drink
Of Darkness finds you by the river-brink,
    And, proffering his Cup, invites your
        Soul
Forth to your Lips to quaff it—do not
    shrink.

OMAR KHAYYÁM

XLVII

And fear not lest Existence closing *your*
Account, should lose, or know the type no
    more ;
    The Eternal Sáki from that Bowl has
        pour'd
Millions of Bubbles like us, and will pour.

XLVIII

When You and I behind the Veil are past,
Oh but the long long while the World
    shall last,
    Which of our Coming and Departure
        heeds
As much as Ocean of a pebble-cast.

OMAR KHAYYÁM

XLIX

One Moment in Annihilation's Waste,
One Moment, of the Well of Life to taste—
  The Stars are setting, and the Caravan
Draws to the Dawn of Nothing—Oh make
    haste !

L

Would you that spangle of Existence
    spend
About THE SECRET—quick about it, Friend !
  A Hair, they say, divides the False and
    True—
And upon what, prithee, does Life depend ?

LI

A Hair, they say, divides the False and
     True;
Yes; and a single Alif were the clue—
  Could you but find it, to the Treasure-
    house,
And peradventure to THE MASTER too;

LII

Whose secret Presence, through Creation's
    veins
Running, Quicksilver-like eludes your
    pains;
  Taking all shapes from Máh to Máhi;
    and
They change and perish all—but He
    remains;

OMAR KHAYYÁM

LIII

A moment guess'd—then back behind the
    Fold
Immerst of Darkness round the Drama
    roll'd
Which, for the Pastime of Eternity,
He does Himself contrive, enact, behold.

LIV

But if in vain, down on the stubborn floor
Of Earth, and up to Heav'n's unopening
    Door,
You gaze To-day, while You are You—
    how then
To-morrow, You when shall be You no
    more?

OMAR KHAYYÁM

LV

Oh, plagued no more with Human or
    Divine,
To-morrow's tangle to itself resign,
    And lose your fingers in the tresses of
The Cypress-slender Minister of Wine.

LVI

Waste not your Hour, nor in the vain
    pursuit
Of This and That endeavour and dispute ;
    Better be merry with the fruitful Grape
Than sadden after none, or bitter, Fruit.

OMAR KHAYYÁM

LVII

You know, my Friends, how bravely in my
 House
For a new Marriage I did make Carouse ;
 Divorced old barren Reason from my
 Bed,
And took the Daughter of the Vine to
 Spouse.

LVIII

For " Is " and " Is-not " though with Rule
 and Line,
And " Up-and-down " by Logic I define,
 Of all that one should care to fathom, I
Was never deep in anything but—Wine.

LIX

Ah, but my Computations, People say,
Have squared the Year to human compass,
    eh ?
  If so, by striking from the Calendar
Unborn To-morrow, and dead Yesterday.

LX

And lately, by the Tavern Door agape,
Came shining through the Dusk an Angel
    Shape
  Bearing a Vessel on his Shoulder; and
He bid me taste of it; and 'twas—the
    Grape !

OMAR KHAYYÁM

LXI

The Grape that can with Logic absolute
The Two-and-Seventy jarring Sects
 confute :
The sovereign Alchemist that in a trice
Life's leaden metal into Gold transmute :

LXII

The mighty Mahmúd, Allah-breathing
 Lord,
That all the misbelieving and black Horde
Of Fears and Sorrows that infest the
 Soul
Scatters before him with his whirlwind
 Sword.

OMAR KHAYYÁM

LXIII

Why, be this Juice the growth of God,
  who dare
Blaspheme the twisted tendril as a Snare?
  A Blessing, we should use it, should we
  not?
And if a Curse—why, then, Who set it
  there?

LXIV

I must abjure the Balm of Life, I must,
Scared by some After-reckoning ta'en on
  trust,
  Or lured with Hope of some Diviner
  Drink,
When the frail Cup is crumbled into Dust!

OMAR KHAYYÁM

LXV

If but the Vine and Love-abjuring Band
Are in the Prophet's Paradise to stand,
   Alack, I doubt the Prophet's Paradise
Were empty as the hollow of one's Hand.

LXVI

Oh threats of Hell and Hopes of Paradise!
One thing at least is certain—*This* Life
    flies ;
   One thing is certain and the rest is Lies ;
The Flower that once is blown for ever
    dies.

OMAR KHAYYÁM

LXVII

Strange, is it not? that of the myriads who
Before us pass'd the door of Darkness
  through,
  Not one returns to tell us of the Road,
Which to discover we must travel too.

LXVIII

The Revelations of Devout and Learn'd
Who rose before us, and as Prophets
  burn'd,
  Are all but Stories, which, awoke from
  Sleep
They told their fellows, and to Sleep
  return'd.

OMAR KHAYYÁM

LXIX

Why, if the Soul can fling the Dust aside,
And naked on the Air of Heaven ride,
   Is't not a Shame—is't not a Shame for
      him
So long in this Clay suburb to abide!

LXX

But that is but a Tent wherein may rest
A Sultán to the realm of Death addrest;
   The Sultán rises, and the dark Ferrásh
Strikes, and prepares it for another Guest.

OMAR KHAYYÁM

LXXI

I sent my Soul through the Invisible,
Some letter of that After-life to spell:
  And after many days my Soul return'd
And said, " Behold, Myself am Heav'n and
      Hell : "

LXXII

Heav'n but the Vision of fulfill'd Desire,
And Hell the Shadow of a Soul on fire,
  Cast on the Darkness into which
      Ourselves,
So late emerged from, shall so soon expire.

OMAR KHAYYÁM

LXXIII

We are no other than a moving row
Of visionary Shapes that come and go
   Round with this Sun-illumined Lantern
      held
In Midnight by the Master of the Show;

LXXIV

Impotent Pieces of the Game He plays
Upon this Chequer-board of Nights and
      Days;
   Hither and thither moves, and checks,
     and slays,
And one by one back in the Closet lays.

OMAR KHAYYÁM

LXXV

The Ball no question makes of Ayes and
     Noes,
But Right or Left as strikes the Player
     goes ;
  And He that toss'd you down into the
     Field,
He knows about it all—HE knows—HE
     knows !

LXXVI

The Moving Finger writes ; and, having
     writ,
Moves on : nor all your Piety nor Wit
  Shall lure it back to cancel half a Line,
Nor all your Tears wash out a Word of it.

OMAR KHAYYÁM

LXXVII

For let Philosopher and Doctor preach
Of what they will, and what they will not
   —each
  Is but one Link in an eternal Chain
That none can slip, nor break, nor over-
  reach.

LXXVIII

And that inverted Bowl we call The Sky,
Whereunder crawling coop'd we live and
   die,
  Lift not your hands to *It* for help—for It
As impotently rolls as you or I.

OMAR KHAYYÁM

LXXIX

With Earth's first Clay They did the Last
    Man knead,
And there of the Last Harvest sow'd the
    Seed:
    And the first Morning of Creation wrote
What the Last Dawn of Reckoning shall
    read.

LXXX

Yesterday, *This* Day's Madness did pre-
    pare:
To-morrow's Silence, Triumph, or Despair:
    Drink! for you know not whence you
    came, nor why:
Drink! for you know not why you go, nor
    where.

OMAR KHAYYÁM

LXXXI

I tell you this—When, started from the
   Goal,
Over the flaming shoulders of the Foal
   Of Heav'n Parwín and Mushtarí they
      flung,
In my predestined Plot of Dust and Soul

LXXXII

The Vine had struck a fibre : which about
If clings my being—let the Dervish flout ;
   Of my Base metal may be filed a Key,
That shall unlock the Door he howls
      without.

OMAR KHAYYÁM

LXXXIII

And this I know: whether the one True
    Light
Kindle to Love, or Wrath-consume me
    quite,
  One Flash of It within the Tavern
    caught
Better than in the Temple lost outright.

LXXXIV

What! out of senseless Nothing to pro-
    voke
A conscious Something to resent the yoke
  Of unpermitted Pleasure, under pain
Of Everlasting Penalties, if broke!

163

OMAR KHAYYÁM

LXXXV

What! from his helpless Creature be
    repaid
Pure Gold for what he lent us dross-allay'd
    Sue for a Debt we never did contract,
And cannot answer—Oh the sorry trade!

LXXXVI

Nay, but, for terror of his wrathful Face,
I swear I will not call Injustice Grace;
    Not one Good Fellow of the Tavern but
Would kick so poor a Coward from the
    place.

OMAR KHAYYÁM

LXXXVII

Oh Thou, who didst with pitfall and with
  gin
Beset the Road I was to wander in,
  Thou wilt not with Predestined Evil
  round
Emmesh, and then impute my Fall to Sin!

LXXXVIII

Oh Thou, who Man of baser Earth didst
  make,
And ev'n with Paradise devise the Snake:
  For all the Sin the Face of wretched
  Man
Is black with—Man's Forgiveness give—
  and take!

* * * * * *

OMAR KHAYYÁM

LXXXIX

As under cover of departing Day
Slunk hunger-stricken Ramazán away,
   Once more within the Potter's house
      alone
I stood, surrounded by the Shapes of Clay.

XC

And once again there gathered a scarce
   heard
Whisper among them; as it were, the
   stirr'd
Ashes of some all but extinguisht Tongue,
Which mine ear kindled into living Word.

XCI

Said one among them—" Surely not in vain,
My substance from the common Earth was
ta'en,
    That He who subtly wrought me into
    Shape
Should stamp me back to shapeless Earth
again ? "

XCII

Another said—" Why, ne'er a peevish Boy
Would break the Cup from which he drank
in Joy;
    Shall He that of His own free Fancy
    made
The Vessel, in an after-rage destroy ! "

OMAR KHAYYÁM

XCIII

None answer'd this; but after silence
    spake
Some Vessel of a more ungainly Make;
    "They sneer at me for leaning all awry;
What! did the Hand then of the Potter
    shake?"

XCIV

Thus with the Dead as with the Living,
    What?
And *Why?* so ready, but the *Wherefor* not,
    One on a sudden peevishly exclaim'd,
"Which is the Potter, pray, and which the
    Pot?"

OMAR KHAYYÁM

XCV

Said one—"Folks of a surly Master tell,
And daub his Visage with the Smoke of
    Hell;
  They talk of some sharp Trial of us—
    Pish!
He's a Good Fellow, and 'twill all be well."

XCVI

"Well," said another, "Whoso will, let try,
My Clay with long oblivion is gone dry:
  But fill me with the old familiar Juice,
Methinks I might recover by-and-bye!"

OMAR KHAYYÁM

XCVII

So while the Vessels one by one were
    speaking,
One spied the little Crescent all were
    seeking:
  And then they jogg'd each other,
    "Brother! Brother!
Now for the Porter's shoulder-knot
    a-creaking!"

   *   *   *   *   *   *

XCVIII

Ah, with the Grape my fading Life provide,
And wash my Body whence the Life has
    died,
  And lay me, shrouded in the living Leaf,
By some not unfrequented Garden-side.

OMAR KHAYYÁM

XCIX

Whither resorting from the vernal Heat
Shall Old Acquaintance Old Acquaintance
      greet,
  Under the Branch that leans above the
      Wall
To shed his Blossom over head and feet.

C

Then ev'n my buried Ashes such a snare
Of Vintage shall fling up into the Air,
  As not a True-believer passing by
But shall be overtaken unaware.

OMAR KHAYYÁM

CI

Indeed the Idols I have loved so long
Have done my credit in Men's eye much
    wrong:
  Have drown'd my Glory in a shallow Cup
And sold my Reputation for a Song.

CII

Indeed, indeed, Repentance oft before
I swore—but was I sober when I swore?
  And then and then came Spring, and
    Rose-in-hand
My thread-bare Penitence apieces tore.

OMAR KHAYYÁM

CIII

And much as Wine has play'd the Infidel,
And robb'd me of my Robe of Honour—
 Well,
 I often wonder what the Vintners buy
One-half so precious as the ware they sell.

CIV

Yet Ah, that Spring should vanish with
 the Rose!
That Youth's sweet-scented manuscript
 should close!
 The Nightingale that in the branches
 sang,
Ah whence, and whither flown again, who
 knows!

OMAR KHAYYÁM

CV

Would but the Desert of the Fountain
    yield
One glimpse—if dimly, yet indeed reveal'd,
  Toward which the fainting Traveller
    might spring,
As springs the trampled herbage of the
    field!

CVI

Oh if the World were but to re-create,
That we might catch ere closed the Book
    of Fate,
  And make The Writer on a fairer leaf
Inscribe our names, or quite obliterate!

OMAR KHAYYÁM

CVII

Better, oh better, cancel from the Scroll
Of Universe one luckless Human Soul,
   Than drop by drop enlarge the Flood
     that rolls
Hoarser with Anguish as the Ages Roll.

CVIII

Ah Love! could you and I with Fate
     conspire
To grasp this sorry Scheme of Things
     entire,
   Would not we shatter it to bits—and
     then
Re-mould it nearer to the Heart's Desire!

OMAR KHAYYÁM

CIX

But see! The rising Moon of Heav'n
  again—
Looks for us, Sweet-heart, through the
  quivering Plane:
How oft hereafter rising will she look
Among those leaves—for one of us in vain!

CX

And when Yourself with silver Foot shall
  pass
Among the Guests Star-scatter'd on the
  Grass,
  And in your joyous errand reach the
  spot
Where I made One—turn down an empty
  Glass!

TAMÁM

X7
LF1